I STAND UP татО BULLIES

WRITTEN BY: MAURICE, CRYSTAL, MYA, CHRISTIAN, AND MAURICE JR., BEAN

ILLUSTRATED BY RICHA KINRA

I Stand Up To Bullies
All Rights Reserved.
Copyright © 2019 Maurice, Crystal, Mya, Christian, and Maurice Jr. Bean
v5.0

This is a work of fiction. The events and characters described herein are imaginary and are not intended to refer to specific places or living persons. The opinions expressed in this manuscript are solely the opinions of the author and do not represent the opinions or thoughts of the publisher. The author has represented and warranted full ownership and/or legal right to publish all the materials in this book.

This book may not be reproduced, transmitted, or stored in whole or in part by any means, including graphic, electronic, or mechanical without the express written consent of the publisher except in the case of brief quotations embodied in critical articles and reviews.

Outskirts Press, Inc.
http://www.outskirtspress.com

ISBN: 978-1-9772-0086-0

Illustrations by Richa Kinra © 2019 Outskirts Press, Inc. All rights reserved - used with permission.

Outskirts Press and the "OP" logo are trademarks belonging to Outskirts Press, Inc.

PRINTED IN THE UNITED STATES OF AMERICA

This Book Belongs to:

Diamond Morris

Life can be so fun. My friends and I play all day together at recess.

We play soccer, dodgeball, and play on the playground. We have no worries in the world except one.

Samuel just cannot seem to be nice to the other kids.
He often says not so nice things.

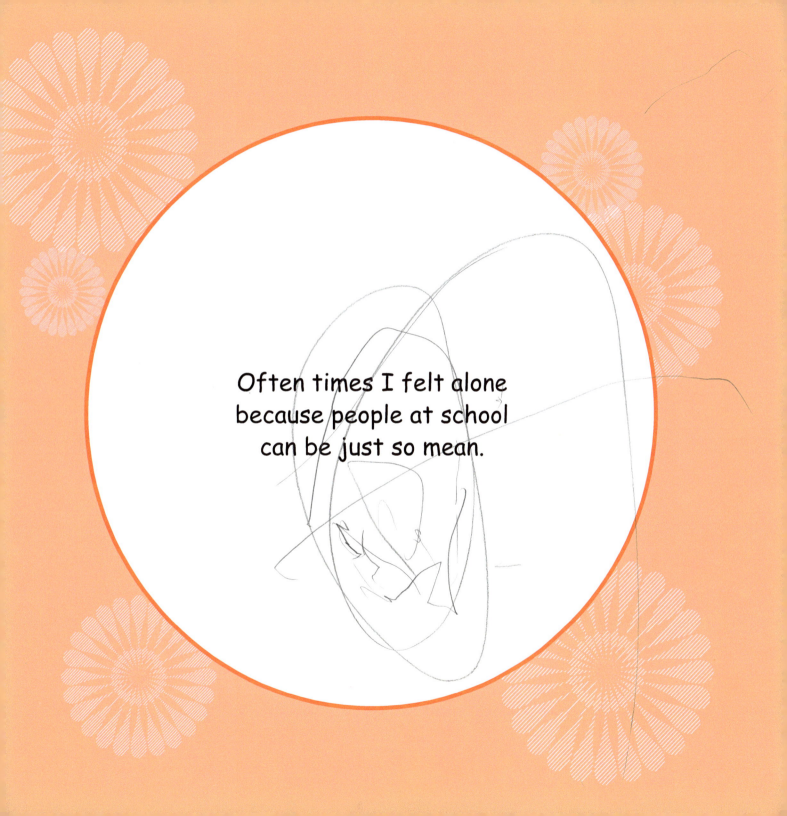

Often times I felt alone because people at school can be just so mean.

Often times I wonder the reason why bullies act the way they do. The only thing I can think of is that someone has bullied them and in return they do the same.

I told myself I would not get bullied anymore, I believe in myself, I love myself, and people should not make me feel sad.

So the next day, I stood up for myself. I told Samuel to stop making fun of me. Every kid is different. It hurts my feelings. I would like you to stop. I feel like I should walk away and never talk to him again.

I did not notice at the time, but I could hear other kids clapping with joy that I stood up for myself.

No matter where you are from and what you look like, others should not make you feel less than who and what you are.

Tomorrow should mark
the beginning of your life.
Be the best you!

CPSIA information can be obtained
at www.ICGtesting.com
Printed in the USA
BVHW021005030719
552419BV00042B/82/P